The Impostures of Scapin

Moliere

Contents

THE IMPOSTURES OF SCAPIN. 9
ACT I. 9
ACT II. 30
ACT III. 61

THE IMPOSTURES OF SCAPIN

BY

Moliere

THE IMPOSTURES OF SCAPIN.

(LES FOURBERIES DE SCAPIN.)

BY

MOLIERE

TRANSLATED INTO ENGLISH PROSE.

WITH SHORT INTRODUCTIONS AND EXPLANATORY NOTES

BY

CHARLES HERON WALL

Acted on May 24, 1671, at the Palais Royal, 'Les Fourberies de Scapin' had great success. It is nothing, however, but a farce, taken partly from classical, partly from Italian or from French sources.

Moliere acted the part of Scapin.

PERSONS REPRESENTED.

ARGANTE, *father to* OCTAVE *and* ZERBINETTE.

GERONTE, *father to* LEANDRE *and* HYACINTHA.

OCTAVE, *son to* ARGANTE, *and lover to* HYACINTHA.

LEANDRE, *son to* GERONTE, *and lover* to ZERBINETTE.

ZERBINETTE, *daughter to* ARGANTE, believed to be a gypsy girl.

HYACINTHA, *daughter to* GERONTE.

SCAPIN, *servant to* LEANDRE.

SILVESTRE, *servant to* OCTAVE.

NERINE, *nurse to* HYACINTHA.

CARLE.

TWO PORTERS.

The scene is at NAPLES.

THE IMPOSTURES OF SCAPIN.

ACT I.

SCENE I.--OCTAVE, SILVESTRE.

OCT. Ah! what sad news for one in love! What a hard fate to be reduced to! So, Silvestre, you have just heard at the harbour that my father is coming back?

SIL. Yes.

OCT. That he returns this very morning?

SIL. This very morning.

OCT. With the intention of marrying me?

SIL. Of marrying you.

OCT. To a daughter of Mr. Geronte?

SIL. Of Mr. Geronte.

OCT. And that this daughter is on her way from Tarentum for that purpose?

SIL. For that purpose.

OCT. And you have this news from my uncle?

SIL. From your uncle.

OCT. To whom my father has given all these particulars in a letter?

SIL. In a letter.

OCT. And this uncle, you say, knows all about our doings?

SIL. All our doings.

OCT. Oh! speak, I pray you; don't go on in such a way as that, and force me to wrench everything from you, word by word.

SIL. But what is the use of my speaking? You don't forget one single detail, but state everything exactly as it is.

OCT. At least advise me, and tell me what I ought to do in this wretched business.

SIL. I really feel as much perplexed as you, and I myself need the advice of some one to guide me.

OCT. I am undone by this unforeseen return.

SIL. And I no less.

OCT. When my father hears what has taken place, a storm of reprimands will burst upon me.

SIL. Reprimands are not very heavy to bear; would to heaven I were free at that price! But I am very likely to pay dearly for all your wild doings, and I see a storm of blows ready to burst upon my shoulders.

OCT. Heavens! how am I to get clear of all the difficulties that beset my path!

SIL. You should have thought of that before entering upon it.

OCT. Oh, don't come and plague me to death with your unreasonable lectures.

SIL. You plague me much more by your foolish deeds.

OCT. What am I to do? What steps must I take? To what course of action have recourse?

SCENE II.--OCTAVE, SCAPIN, SILVESTRE.

SCA. How now, Mr. Octave? What is the matter with you? What is it? What trouble are you in? You are all upset, I see.

OCT. Ah! my dear Scapin, I am in despair; I am lost; I am the most unfortunate of mortals.

SCA. How is that?

OCT. Don't you know anything of what has happened to me?

SCA. No.

OCT. My father is just returning with Mr. Geronte, and they want to marry me.

SCA. Well, what is there so dreadful about that?

OCT. Alas! you don't know what cause I have to be anxious.

SCA. No; but it only depends on you that I should soon know; and I am a man of consolation, a man who can interest himself in the troubles of young people.

OCT. Ah! Scapin, if you could find some scheme, invent some plot, to get me out of the trouble I am in, I should think myself indebted to you for more than life.

SCA. To tell you the truth, there are few things impossible to me when I once set about them. Heaven has bestowed on me a fair enough share of genius for the making up of all those neat strokes of mother wit, for all those ingenious gallantries to which the ignorant and vulgar give the name of impostures; and I can boast, without vanity, that there have been very few men more skilful than I in expedients and intrigues, and who have acquired a greater reputation in the noble profession. But, to tell the truth, merit is too ill rewarded nowadays, and I have given up everything of the kind since the trouble I had through a certain affair which happened to me.

OCT. How? What affair, Scapin?

SCA. An adventure in which justice and I fell out.

OCT. Justice and you?

SCA. Yes; we had a trifling quarrel.

SIL. You and justice?

SCA. Yes. She used me very badly; and I felt so enraged against the ingratitude of our age that I determined never to do anything for anybody. But never mind; tell me about yourself all the same.

OCT. You know, Scapin, that two months ago Mr. Geronte and my father set out together on a voyage, about a certain business in which they are both interested.

SCA. Yes, I know that.

OCT. And that both Leandre and I were left by our respective fathers, I under the management of Silvestre, and Leandre under your management.

SCA. Yes; I have acquitted myself very well of my charge.

OCT. Some time afterwards Leandre met with a young gipsy girl, with whom he fell in love.

SCA. I know that too.

OCT. As we are great friends, he told me at once of his love, and took me to see this young girl, whom I thought good-looking, it is true, but not so beautiful as he would have had me believe. He never spoke of anything but her; at every opportunity he exaggerated her grace and her beauty, extolled her intelligence, spoke to me with transport of the charms of her conversation, and related to me her most insignificant saying, which he always wanted me to think the cleverest thing in the world. He often found fault with me for not thinking as highly as he imagined I ought to do of the things he related to me, and blamed me again and again for being so insensible to the power of love.

SCA. I do not see what you are aiming at in all this.

OCT. One day, as I was going with him to the people who have charge of the girl with whom he is in love, we heard in a small house on a by-street, lamentations mixed with a good deal of sobbing. We inquired what it was, and were told by a woman that we might see there a most piteous sight, in the persons of two strangers, and that unless we were quite insensible to pity, we should be sure to be touched with it.

SCA. Where will this lead to?

OCT. Curiosity made me urge Leandre to come in with me. We went into a low room, where we saw an old woman dying, and with her a servant who was uttering lamentations, and a young girl dissolved in tears, the most beautiful, the most touching sight that you ever saw.

SCA. Oh! oh!

OCT. Any other person would have seemed frightful in the condition she was in, for all the dress she had on was a scanty old petticoat, with a night jacket of plain fustian, and turned back at the top of her head a yellow cap, which let her hair fall in disorder on her shoulders; and yet dressed even thus she shone with a thousand attractions, and all her person was most charming and pleasant.

SCA. I begin to understand.

OCT. Had you but seen her, Scapin, as I did, you would have thought her admirable.

SCA. Oh! I have no doubt about it; and without seeing her, I plainly perceive that she must have been altogether charming.

OCT. Her tears were none of those unpleasant tears which spoil the face; she had a most touching grace in weeping, and her sorrow was a most beautiful thing to witness.

SCA. I can see all that.

OCT. All who approached her burst into tears whilst she threw herself, in her loving way, on the body of the dying woman, whom she called her dear mother; and nobody could help being moved to the depths of the heart to see a girl with such a loving disposition.

SCA. Yes, all that is very touching; and I understand that this loving disposition made you love her.

OCT. Ah! Scapin, a savage would have loved her.

SCA. Certainly; how could anyone help doing so?

OCT. After a few words, with which I tried to soothe her grief, we left her; and when I asked Leandre what he thought of her, he answered coldly that she was rather pretty! I was wounded to find how unfeelingly he spoke to me of her, and I would not tell him the effect her beauty had had on my heart.

SIL. (*to* OCTAVE). If you do not abridge your story, we shall have to stop here till to-morrow. Leave it to me to finish it in a few words. (*To* SCAPIN) His heart takes fire from that moment. He cannot live without going to comfort the amiable and sorrowful girl. His frequent visits are forbidden by the servant, who has become her guardian by the death of the mother. Our young man is in despair; he presses, begs, beseeches--all in vain. He is told that the young girl, although without friends and without fortune, is of an honourable family, and that, unless he marries her, he must cease his visits. His love increases with the difficulties. He racks his brains; debates, reasons, ponders, and makes up his mind. And, to cut a long story short, he has been married these three days.

SCA. I see.

SIL. Now, add to this the unforeseen return of the father, who was not to be back before two whole months; the discovery which the uncle has made of the marriage; and that other marriage projected between him and a daughter which Mr. Geronte had by a second wife, whom, they say, he married at Tarentum.

OCT. And, above all, add also the poverty of my beloved, and the impossibility there is for me to do anything for her relief.

SCA. Is that all? You are both of you at a great loss about nothing. Is there any reason to be alarmed? Are you not ashamed, you, Silvestre, to fall short in such a small matter? Deuce take it all! You, big and stout as father and mother put together, you can't find any expedient in your noddle? you can't plan any stratagem, invent any gallant intrigue to put matters straight? Fie! Plague on the booby! I wish I had had the two old fellows to bamboozle in former times; I should not have thought much of it; and I was no bigger than that, when I had given a hundred delicate proofs of my skill.

SIL. I acknowledge that Heaven has not given me your talent, and that I have not the brains like you to embroil myself with justice.

OCT. Here is my lovely Hyacintha!

SCENE III.--HYACINTHA, OCTAVE, SCAPIN, SILVESTRE.

HYA. Ah! Octave, is what Silvestre has just told Nerine really true? Is your father back, and is he bent upon marrying you?

OCT. Yes, it is so, dear Hyacintha; and these tidings have given me a cruel shock. But what do I see? You are weeping? Why those tears? Do you suspect me of unfaithfulness, and have you no assurance of the love I feel for you?

HYA. Yes, Octave, I am sure that you love me now; but can I be sure that you will love me always?

OCT. Ah! could anyone love you once without loving you for ever?

HYA. I have heard say, Octave, that your sex does not love so long as ours, and that the ardour men show is a fire which dies out as easily as it is kindled.

OCT. Then, my dear Hyacintha, my heart is not like that of other men, and I feel certain that I shall love you till I die.

HYA. I want to believe what you say, and I have no doubt that you are sincere; but I fear a power which will oppose in your heart the tender feelings you have for me. You depend on a father who would marry you to another, and I am sure it would kill me if such a thing happened.

OCT. No, lovely Hyacintha, there is no father who can force me to break my faith to you, and I could resolve to leave my country, and even to die, rather than be separated from you. Without having seen her, I have already conceived a horrible aversion to her whom they want me to marry; and although I am not cruel, I wish the sea would swallow her up, or drive her hence forever. Do not weep, then, dear Hyacintha, for your tears kill me, and I cannot see them without feeling pierced to the heart.

HYA. Since you wish it, I will dry my tears, and I will wait without fear for what Heaven shall decide.

OCT. Heaven will be favourable to us.

HYA. It cannot be against us if you are faithful.

OCT. I certainly shall be so.

HYA. Then I shall be happy.

SCA. (*aside*). She is not so bad, after all, and I think her pretty enough.

OCT. (*showing* SCAPIN). Here is a man who, if he would, could be of the greatest help to us in all our trouble.

SCA. I have sworn with many oaths never more to meddle with anything. But if you both entreat me very much, I might....

OCT. Ah! if entreaties will obtain your help, I beseech you with all my heart to steer our bark.

SCA. (*to* HYACINTHA). And you, have you anything to say?

HYA. Like him, I beseech you, by all that is most dear to you upon earth, to assist us in our love.

SCA. I must have a little humanity, and give way. There, don't be afraid; I will do all I can for you.

OCT. Be sure that....

SCA. (*to* OCTAVE). Hush! (*To* HYACINTHA) Go, and make yourself easy.

SCENE IV.--OCTAVE, SCAPIN, SILVESTRE.

SCA. (*to* OCTAVE). You must prepare yourself to receive your father with firmness.

OCT. I confess that this meeting frightens me before hand, for with him I have a natural shyness that I cannot conquer.

SCA. Yes; you must be firm from the first, for fear that he should take advantage of your weakness, and lead you like a child. Now, come, try to school yourself into some amount of firmness, and be ready to answer boldly all he can say to you.

OCT. I will do the best I can.

SCA. Well! let us try a little, just to see. Rehearse your part, and let us see how you will manage. Come, a look of decision, your head erect, a bold face.

OCT. Like this.

SCA. A little more.

OCT. So?

SCA. That will do. Now, fancy that I am your father, just arrived; answer me boldly as if it were he himself.--"What! you scoundrel, you good-for-nothing fellow, you infamous rascal, unworthy son of such a father as I, dare you appear before me after what you have done, and after the infamous trick you have played me during my absence? Is this, you rascal, the reward of all my care? Is this the fruit of all my devotion? Is this the respect due to me? Is this the respect you retain for me?"--Now then, now then.--"You are insolent enough, scoundrel, to go and engage yourself without the consent of your father, and contract a clandestine marriage! Answer me, you villain! Answer me. Let me hear your fine reasons"....--Why, the deuce, you seem quite lost.

OCT. It is because I imagine I hear my father speaking.

SCA. Why, yes; and it is for this reason that you must try not to look like an idiot.

OCT. I will be more resolute, and will answer more firmly.

SCA. Quite sure?

SIL. Here is your father coming.

OCT. Oh heavens! I am lost.

SCENE V.--SCAPIN, SILVESTRE.

SCA. Stop, Octave; stop. He's off. What a poor specimen it is! Let's wait for the old man all the same.

SIL. What shall I tell him?

SCA. Leave him to me; only follow me.

SCENE VI.--ARGANTE, SCAPIN, SILVESTRE (at the further part of the stage).

ARG. (*thinking himself alone*). Did anyone ever hear of such an action?

SCA. (*to* SILVESTRE). He has already heard of the affair, and is so struck by it that, although alone, he speaks aloud about it.

ARG. (*thinking himself alone*). Such a bold thing to do.

SCA. (*to* SILVESTRE). Let us listen to him.

ARG. (*thinking himself alone*). I should like to know what they can say to me about this fine marriage.

SCA. (*aside*). We have it all ready.

ARG. (*thinking himself alone*). Will they try to deny it?

SCA. (*aside*). No: we have no thought of doing so.

ARG. (*thinking himself alone*). Or will they undertake to excuse it?

SCA. (*aside*). That may be.

ARG. (*thinking himself alone*). Do they intend to deceive me with impertinent stories?

SCA. (*aside*). May be.

ARG. (*thinking himself alone*). All they can say will be useless.

SCA. We shall see.

ARG. (*thinking himself alone*). They will not take me in.

SCA. (*aside*). I don't know that.

ARG. (*thinking himself alone*). I shall know how to put my rascal of a son in a safe place.

SCA. (*aside*). We shall see about that.

ARG. (*thinking himself alone*). And as for that rascal

Silvestre, I will cudgel him soundly.

SIL. (*to* SCAPIN). I should have been very much astonished if he had forgotten me.

ARG. (*seeing* SILVESTRE). Ah, ah! here you are, most wise governor of a family, fine director of young people!

SCA. Sir, I am delighted to see you back.

ARG. Good morning, Scapin. (*To* SILVESTRE) You have really followed my orders in a fine manner, and my son has behaved splendidly.

SCA. You are quite well, I see.

ARG. Pretty well. (*To* SILVESTRE) You don't say a word, you rascal!

SCA. Have you had a pleasant journey?

ARG. Yes, yes, very good. Leave me alone a little to scold this villain!

SCA. You want to scold?

ARG. Yes, I wish to scold.

SCA. But whom, Sir?

ARG. (*Pointing to* SILVESTRE). This scoundrel!

SCA. Why?

ARG. Have you not heard what has taken place during my absence?

SCA. Yes, I have heard some trifling thing.

ARG. How! Some trifling thing! Such an action as this?

SCA. You are about right.

ARG. Such a daring thing to do!

SCA. That's quite true.

ARG. To marry without his father's consent!

SCA. Yes, there is something to be said against it, but my opinion is that you should make no fuss about it.

ARG. This is your opinion, but not mine; and I will make as much fuss as I please. What! do you not think that I have every reason to be angry?

SCA. Quite so. I was angry myself when I first heard it; and I so far felt interested in your behalf that I rated your son well. Just ask him the fine sermons I gave him, and how I lectured him about the little respect he showed his father, whose very footsteps he ought to kiss. You could not yourself talk better to him. But what of that? I submitted to reason, and considered that, after all, he had done nothing so dreadful.

ARG. What are you telling me? He has done nothing so dreadful? When he goes and marries straight off a perfect stranger?

SCA. What can one do? he was urged to it by his destiny.

ARG. Oh, oh! You give me there a fine reason. One has nothing better to do now than to commit the greatest crime imaginable--to cheat, steal, and murder--and give for an excuse that we were urged to it by destiny.

SCA. Ah me! You take my words too much like a philosopher. I mean to say that he was fatally engaged in this affair.

ARG. And why did he engage in it?

SCA. Do you expect him to be as wise as you are? Can you put an old head on young shoulders, and expect young people to have all the prudence necessary to do nothing but what is reasonable? Just look at our Leandre, who, in spite of all my lessons, has done even worse than that. I should like to know whether you yourself were not young once, and have not played as many pranks as others? I have heard say that you were a sad fellow in your time, that you played the gallant among the most gallant of those days, and that you never gave in until you had gained your point.

ARG. It is true, I grant it; but I always confined myself to gallantry, and never went so far as to do what he has done.

SCA. But what was he to do? He sees a young person who wishes him well; for he inherits it from you that all women love him. He thinks her charming, goes to see her, makes love to her, sighs as lovers sigh, and does the passionate swain. She yields to his pressing visits; he pushes his fortune. But her relations catch him with her, and oblige him to marry her by main force.

SIL. (*aside*). What a clever cheat!

SCA. Would you have him suffer them to murder him? It is still better to be married than to be dead.

ARG. I was not told that the thing had happened in that way.

SCA. (*showing* SILVESTRE). Ask him, if you like; he will tell you the same thing.

ARG. (*to* SILVESTRE). Was he married against his wish?

SIL. Yes, Sir.

SCA. Do you think I would tell you an untruth?

ARG. Then he should have gone at once to a lawyer to protest against the violence.

SCA. It is the very thing he would not do.

ARG. It would have made it easier for me to break off the marriage.

SCA. Break off the marriage?

ARG. Yes

SCA. You will not break it off.

ARG. I shall not break it off?

SCA. No.

ARG. What! Have I not on my side the rights of a father, and can I not have satisfaction for the violence done to my son?

SCA. This is a thing he will not consent to.

ARG. He will not consent to it?

SCA. No.

ARG. My son?

SCA. Your son. Would you have him acknowledge that he was frightened, and that he yielded by force to what was wanted of him? He will take care not to confess that; it would be to wrong himself, and show himself unworthy of a father like you.

ARG. I don't care for all that.

SCA. He must, for his own honour and yours, say that he married of his own free will.

ARG. And I wish for my own honour, and for his, that he should say the contrary.

SCA. I am sure he will not do that.

ARG. I shall soon make him do it.

SCA. He will not acknowledge it, I tell you.

ARG. He shall do it, or I will disinherit him.

SCA. You?

ARG. I.

SCA. Nonsense!

ARG. How nonsense?

SCA. You will not disinherit him.

ARG. I shall not disinherit him?

SCA. No.

ARG. No?

SCA. No.

ARG. Well! This is really too much! I shall not disinherit my son!

SCA. No, I tell you.

ARG. Who will hinder me?

SCA. You yourself.

ARG. I?

SCA. Yes; you will never have the heart to do it.

ARG. I shall have the heart.

SCA. You are joking.

ARG. I am not joking.

SCA. Paternal love will carry the day.

ARG. No, it will not.

SCA. Yes, yes.

ARG. I tell you that I will disinherit him.

SCA. Rubbish.

ARG. You may say rubbish; but I will.

SCA. Gracious me, I know that you are naturally a kind-hearted man.

ARG. No, I am not kind-hearted; I can be angry when I choose. Leave off talking; you put me out of all patience. (*To* SYLVESTRE) Go, you rascal, run and fetch my son, while I go to Mr. Geronte and tell him of my misfortune.

SCA. Sir, if I can be useful to you in any way, you have but to order me.

ARG. I thank you. (*Aside*) Ah! Why is he my only son? Oh! that I had with me the daughter that Heaven has taken away from me, so that I might make her my heir.

SCENE VII.--SCAPIN, SYLVESTRE.

SIL. You are a great man, I must confess; and things are in a fair way to succeed. But, on the other hand, we are greatly pressed for money, and we have people dunning us.

SCA. Leave it to me; the plan is all ready. I am only puzzling my brains to find out a fellow to act along with us, in order to play a personage I want. But let me see; just look at me a little. Stick your cap rather rakishly on one side. Put on a furious look. Put your hand on your side. Walk about like a king on the stage. [Footnote: Compare the 'Impromptu of Versailles'.] That will do. Follow me. I possess some means of changing your face and voice.

SIL. I pray you, Scapin, don't go and embroil me with justice.

SCA. Never mind, we will share our perils like brothers, and three years more or less on the galleys are not sufficient to check a noble heart.

ACT II.

SCENE I.--GERONTE, ARGANTE.

GER. Yes, there is no doubt but that with this weather we shall have our people with us to-day; and a sailor who has arrived from Tarentum told me just now that he had seen our man about to start with the ship. But my daughter's arrival will find things strangely altered from what we thought they would be, and what you have just told me of your son has put an end to all the plans we had made together.

ARG. Don't be anxious about that; I give you my word that I shall remove that obstacle, and I am going to see about it this moment.

GER. In all good faith, Mr. Argante, shall I tell you what? The education of children is a thing that one could never be too careful about.

ARG. You are right; but why do you say that?

GER. Because most of the follies of young men come from the way they have been brought up by their fathers.

ARG. It is so sometimes, certainly; but what do you mean by saying that to me?

GER. Why do I say that to you?

ARG. Yes.

GER. Because, if, like a courageous father, you had corrected your son when he was young, he would not have played you such a trick.

ARG. I see. So that you have corrected your own much better?

GER. Certainly; and I should be very sorry if he had done anything at all like what yours has done.

ARG. And if that son, so well brought up, had done worse even than mine, what would you say?

GER. What?

ARG. What?

GER. What do you mean?

ARG. I mean, Mr. Geronte, that we should never be so ready to blame the conduct of others, and that those who live in glass houses should not throw stones.

GER. I really do not understand you.

ARG. I will explain myself.

GER. Have you heard anything about my son?

ARG. Perhaps I have.

GER. But what?

ARG. Your servant Scapin, in his vexation, only told me the thing roughly, and you can learn all the particulars from him or from some one else. For my part, I will at once go to my solicitor, and see what steps I can take in the matter. Good-bye.

SCENE II.--GERONTE (*alone*).

GER. What can it be? Worse than what his son has done! I am sure I don't know what anyone can do more wrong than that; and to marry without the consent of one's father is the worst thing that I can possibly imagine. [Footnote: No exaggeration, if we consider that this was said two hundred years ago, and by a French father.]

SCENE III--GERONTE, LEANDRE.

GER. Ah, here you are!

LEA. (*going quickly towards his father to embrace him*). Ah! father, how glad I am to see you!

GER. (*refusing to embrace him*). Stay, I have to speak to you first.

LEA. Allow me to embrace you, and....

GER. (*refusing him again*). Gently, I tell you.

LEA. How! father, you deprive me of the pleasure of showing you my joy at your return?

GER. Certainly; we have something to settle first of all.

LEA. But what?

GER. Just stand there before me, and let me look at you.

LEA. What for?

GER. Look me straight in the face.

LEA. Well?

GER. Will you tell me what has taken place here in my absence?

LEA. What has taken place?

GER. Yes; what did you do while I was away?

LEA. What would you have me do, father?

GER. It is not I who wanted you to do anything, but who ask you now what it is you did?

LEA. I have done nothing to give you reason to complain.

GER. Nothing at all?

LEA. No.

GER. You speak in a very decided tone.

LEA. It is because I am innocent.

GER. And yet Scapin has told me all about you.

LEA. Scapin!

GER. Oh! oh! that name makes you change colour.

LEA. He has told you something about me?

GER. He has. But this is not the place to talk about the business, and we must go elsewhere to see to it. Go home at once; I will be there presently. Ah! scoundrel, if you mean to bring dishonour upon me, I will renounce you for my son, and you will have to avoid my presence for ever!

SCENE IV.--LEANDRE (*alone*).

LEA. To betray me after that fashion! A rascal who for so many reasons should be the first to keep secret what I trust him with! To go and tell everything to my father! Ah! I swear by all that is dear to me not to let such villainy go unpunished.

SCENE V.--OCTAVE, LEANDRE, SCAPIN.

OCT. My dear Scapin, what do I not owe to you? What a wonderful man you are, and how kind of Heaven to send you to my help!

LEA. Ah, ah! here you are, you rascal!

SCA. Sir, your servant; you do me too much honour.

LEA. (*drawing his sword*). You are setting me at defiance, I believe...Ah! I will teach you how....

SCA. (*falling on his knees*). Sir!

OCT. (*stepping between them*). Ah! Leandre.

LEA. No, Octave, do not keep me back.

SCA. (*to* LEANDRE). Eh! Sir.

OCT. (*keeping back* LEANDRE). For mercy's sake!

LEA. (*trying to strike*). Leave me to wreak my anger upon him.

OCT. In the name of our friendship, Leandre, do not strike him.

SCA. What have I done to you, Sir?

LEA. What you have done, you scoundrel!

OCT. (*still keeping back* LEANDRE). Gently, gently.

LEA. No, Octave, I will have him confess here on the spot the perfidy of which he is guilty. Yes, scoundrel, I know the trick you have played me; I have just been told of it. You did not think the secret would be revealed to me, did you? But I will have you confess it with your own lips, or I will run you through and through with my sword.

SCA. Ah! Sir, could you really be so cruel as that?

LEA. Speak, I say.

SCA. I have done something against you, Sir?

LEA. Yes, scoundrel! and your conscience must tell you only too well what it is.

SCA. I assure you that I do not know what you mean.

LEA. (*going towards* SCAPIN *to strike him*). You do not know?

OCT. (*keeping back* LEANDRE). Leandre!

SCA. Well, Sir, since you will have it, I confess that I drank with some of my friends that small cask of Spanish wine you received as a present some days ago, and that it was I who made that opening in the cask, and spilled some water on the ground round it, to make you believe that all the wine had leaked out.

LEA. What! scoundrel, it was you who drank my Spanish wine, and who suffered me to scold the servant so much, because I thought it was she who had played me that trick?

SCA. Yes, Sir; I am very sorry, Sir.

LEA. I am glad to know this. But this is not what I am about now.

SCA. It is not that, Sir?

LEA. No; it is something else, for which I care much more, and I will have you tell it me.

SCA. I do not remember, Sir, that I ever did anything else.

LEA. (*trying to strike* SCAPIN). Will you speak?

SCA. Ah!

OCT. (*keeping back* LEANDRE). Gently.

SCA. Yes, Sir; it is true that three weeks ago, when you sent me in the evening to take a small watch to the gypsy [Footnote: *Egyptienne*. Compare act v. scene ii. *Bohemienne* is a more usual name.] girl you love, and I came back, my clothes spattered with mud and my face covered with blood, I told you that I had been attacked by robbers who had beaten me soundly and had stolen the watch from me. It is true that I told a lie. It was I who kept the watch, Sir.

LEA. It was you who stole the watch?

SCA. Yes, Sir, in order to know the time.

LEA. Ah! you are telling me fine things; I have indeed a very faithful servant! But it is not this that I want to know of you.

SCA. It is not this?

LEA. No, infamous wretch! it is something else that I want you to confess.

SCA. (*aside*). Mercy on me!

LEA. Speak at once; I will not be put off.

SCA. Sir, I have done nothing else.

LEA. (*trying to strike* SCAPIN). Nothing else?

OCT. (*stepping between them*). Ah! I beg....

SCA. Well, Sir, you remember that ghost that six months ago cudgelled you soundly, and almost made you break your neck down a cellar, where you fell whilst running away?

LEA. Well?

SCA. It was I, Sir, who was playing the ghost.

LEA. It was you, wretch! who were playing the ghost?

SCA. Only to frighten you a little, and to cure you of the habit of making us go out every night as you did.

LEA. I will remember in proper time and place all I have just heard. But I'll have you speak about the present matter, and tell me what it is you said to my father.

SCA. What I said to your father?

LEA. Yes, scoundrel! to my father.

SCA. Why, I have not seen him since his return!

LEA. You have not seen him?

SCA. No, Sir.

LEA. Is that the truth?

SCA. The perfect truth; and he shall tell you so himself.

LEA. And yet it was he himself who told me.

SCA. With your leave, Sir, he did not tell you the truth.

SCENE VI.--LEANDRE, OCTAVE, CARLE, SCAPIN.

CAR. Sir, I bring you very bad news concerning your love affair.

LEA. What is it now?

CAR. The gypsies are on the point of carrying off Zerbinette. She came herself all in tears to ask me to tell you that, unless you take to them, before two hours are over, the money they have asked you for her, she will be lost to you for ever.

LEA. Two hours?

CAR. Two hours.

SCENE VII.--LEANDRE, OCTAVE, SCAPIN.

LEA. Ah! my dear Scapin, I pray you to help me.

SCA. (*rising and passing proudly before* LEANDRE). Ah! my dear Scapin! I am my dear Scapin, now that I am wanted.

LEA. I will forgive you all that you confessed just now, and more also.

SCA. No, no; forgive me nothing; run your sword through and through my body. I should be perfectly satisfied if you were to kill me.

LEA. I beseech you rather to give me life by serving my love.

SCA. Nay, nay; better kill me.

LEA. You are too dear to me for that. I beg of you to make use for me of that wonderful genius of yours which can conquer everything.

SCA. Certainly not. Kill me, I tell you.

LEA. Ah! for mercy's sake, don't think of that now, but try to give me the help I ask.

OCT. Scapin, you must do something to help him.

SCA. How can I after such abuse?

LEA. I beseech you to forget my outburst of temper, and to make use of your skill for me.

OCT. I add my entreaties to his.

SCA. I cannot forget such an insult.

OCT. You must not give way to resentment, Scapin.

LEA. Could you forsake me, Scapin, in this cruel extremity?

SCA. To come all of a sudden and insult me like that.

LEA. I was wrong, I acknowledge.

SCA. To call me scoundrel, knave, infamous wretch!

LEA. I am really very sorry.

SCA. To wish to send your sword through my body!

LEA. I ask you to forgive me, with all my heart; and if you want to see me at your feet, I beseech you, kneeling, not to give me up.

OCT. Scapin, you cannot resist that?

SCA. Well, get up, and another time remember not to be so hasty.

LEA. Will you try to act for me?

SCA. I will see.

LEA. But you know that time presses.

SCA. Don't be anxious. How much is it you want?

LEA. Five hundred crowns.

SCA. You?

OCT. Two hundred pistoles.

SCA. I must extract this money from your respective fathers' pockets. (*To* OCTAVE) As far as yours is concerned, my plan is all ready. (*To* LEANDRE) And as for yours, although he is the greatest miser imaginable, we shall find it easier still; for you know that he is not blessed with too much intellect, and I look upon him as a man who will believe anything. This cannot offend you; there is not a suspicion of a resemblance between him and you; and you know what the world thinks, that he is your father only in name.

LEA. Gently, Scapin.

SCA. Besides, what does it matter? But, Mr. Octave, I see your father coming. Let us begin by him, since he is the first to cross our path.

Vanish both of you; (*to* OCTAVE) and you, please, tell Silvestre to come quickly, and take his part in the affair.

SCENE VIII.--ARGANTE, SCAPIN.

SCA. (*aside*). Here he is, turning it over in his mind.

ARG. (*thinking himself alone*). Such behaviour and such lack of consideration! To entangle himself in an engagement like that! Ah! rash youth.

SCA. Your servant, Sir.

ARG. Good morning, Scapin.

SCA. You are thinking of your son's conduct.

ARG. Yes, I acknowledge that it grieves me deeply.

SCA. Ah! Sir, life is full of troubles; and we should always be prepared for them. I was told, a long time ago, the saying of an ancient philosopher which I have never forgotten.

ARG. What was it?

SCA. That if the father of a family has been away from home for ever so short a time, he ought to dwell upon all the sad news that may greet him on his return. He ought to fancy his house burnt down, his money stolen, his wife dead, his son married, his daughter ruined; and be very thankful for whatever falls short of all this. In my small way of philosophy, I have ever taken this lesson to heart; and I never come home but I expect to have to bear with the anger of my masters, their scoldings, insults, kicks, blows, and horse-whipping. And I always thank my destiny for whatever I do not receive.

ARG. That's all very well; but this rash marriage is more than I can put up with, and it forces me to break off the match I had intended for my son. I have come from my solicitor's to see if we can cancel it.

SCA. Well, Sir, if you will take my advice, you will look to some other way of settling this business. You know what a law-suit means in this country, and you'll find yourself in the midst of a strange bush of thorns.

ARG. I am fully aware that you are quite right; but what else can I do?

SCA. I think I have found something that will answer much better. The sorrow that I felt for you made me rummage in my head to find some means of getting you out of trouble; for I cannot bear to see kind fathers a prey to grief without feeling sad about it, and, besides, I have at all times had the greatest regard for you.

ARG. I am much obliged to you.

SCA. Then you must know that I went to the brother of the young girl whom your son has married. He is one of those fire-eaters, one of those men all sword-thrusts, who speak of nothing but fighting, and who think no more of killing a man than of swallowing a glass of wine. I got him to speak of this marriage; I showed him how easy it would be to have it broken off, because of the violence used towards your son. I spoke to him of your prerogatives as father, and of the weight which your rights, your money, and your friends would have with justice. I managed him so that at last he lent a ready ear to the propositions I made to him of arranging the matter amicably for a sum of money. In short, he will give his consent to the marriage being cancelled, provided you pay him well.

ARG. And how much did he ask?

SCA. Oh! at first things utterly out of the question.

ARG. But what?

SCA. Things utterly extravagant.

ARG. But what?

SCA. He spoke of no less than five or six hundred pistoles.

ARG. Five or six hundred agues to choke him withal. Does he think me a fool?

SCA. Just what I told him. I laughed his proposal to scorn, and made him understand that you were not a man to be duped in that fashion, and of whom anyone can ask five or six hundred pistoles! However, after much talking, this is what we decided upon. "The time is now come," he said, "when I must go and rejoin the army. I am buying my equipments, and the want of money I am in forces me to listen to what you propose. I must have a horse, and I cannot obtain one at all fit for the service under sixty pistoles."

ARG. Well, yes; I am willing to give sixty pistoles.

SCA. He must have the harness and pistols, and that will cost very nearly twenty pistoles more.

ARG. Twenty and sixty make eighty.

SCA. Exactly.

ARG. It's a great deal; still, I consent to that.

SCA. He must also have a horse for his servant, which, we may expect, will cost at least thirty pistoles.

ARG. How, the deuce! Let him go to Jericho. He shall have nothing at all.

SCA. Sir!

ARG. No; he's an insolent fellow.

SCA. Would you have his servant walk?

ARG. Let him get along as he pleases, and the master too.

SCA. Now, Sir, really don't go and hesitate for so little. Don't have recourse to law, I beg of you, but rather give all that is asked of you, and save yourself from the clutches of justice.

ARG. Well, well! I will bring myself to give these thirty pistoles also.

SCA. "I must also have," he said, "a mule to carry...."

ARG. Let him go to the devil with his mule! This is asking too much. We will go before the judges.

SCA. I beg of you, Sir!

ARG. No, I will not give in.

SCA. Sir, only one small mule.

ARG. No; not even an ass.

SCA. Consider....

ARG. No, I tell you; I prefer going to law.

SCA. Ah! Sir, what are you talking about, and what a resolution you are going to take. Just cast a glance on the ins and outs of justice, look at the number of appeals, of stages of jurisdiction; how many embarrassing procedures; how many ravening wolves through whose claws you will have to pass; serjeants, solicitors, counsel, registrars, substitutes, recorders, judges and their clerks. There is not one of these who, for the merest trifle, couldn't knock over the best case in the world. A serjeant will issue false writs without your knowing anything of it. Your solicitor will act in concert with your adversary, and sell you for ready money. Your counsel, bribed in the same way, will be nowhere to be found when your case comes on, or else will bring forward arguments which are the merest shooting in the air, and will never come to the point. The registrar will issue writs and decrees against you for contumacy. The recorder's clerk will make away with some of your papers, or the instructing officer himself will not say what he has seen, and when, by dint of the wariest possible precautions, you have escaped all these traps, you will be amazed that your judges have been set against you either by bigots or by the women they love. Ah! Sir, save yourself from such a hell, if you can. 'Tis damnation in this world to have to go to law;

and the mere thought of a lawsuit is quite enough to drive me to the other end of the world.

ARG. How much does he want for the mule?

SCA. For the mule, for his horse and that of his servant, for the harness and pistols, and to pay a little something he owes at the hotel, he asks altogether two hundred pistoles, Sir.

ARG. Two hundred pistoles?

SCA. Yes.

ARG. (*walking about angrily*). No, no; we will go to law.

SCA. Recollect what you are doing.

ARG. I shall go to law.

SCA. Don't go and expose yourself to....

ARG. I will go to law.

SCA. But to go to law you need money. You must have money for the summons, you must have money for the rolls, for prosecution, attorney's introduction, solicitor's advice, evidence, and his days in court. You must have money for the consultations and pleadings of the counsel, for the right of withdrawing the briefs, and for engrossed copies of the documents. You must have money for the reports of the substitutes, for the court fees [1] at the conclusion, for registrar's enrolment, drawing up of deeds, sentences, decrees, rolls, signings, and clerks' despatches; letting alone all the presents you will have to make. Give this money to the man, and there you are well out of the whole thing.

[1] *Epices*, "spices," in ancient times, equalled *sweetmeats*, and were given to the judge by the side which gained the suit, as a mark of gratitude. These *epices* had long been changed into a compulsory payment of money when Moliere wrote. In Racine's ***Plaideurs***, act ii. scene vii., Petit Jean takes literally the demand of the judge for *epices*, and fetches the pepper-box to satisfy him.

ARG. Two hundred pistoles!

SCA. Yes, and you will save by it. I have made a small calculation in my head of all that justice costs, and I find that by giving two hundred pistoles to your man you will have a large margin left--say, at least a hundred and fifty pistoles--without taking into consideration the cares, troubles, and anxieties, which you will spare yourself. For were it only to avoid being before everybody the butt of some facetious counsel, I had rather give three hundred pistoles than go to law. [Footnote: What would Moliere have said if he had been living now!]

ARG. I don't care for that, and I challenge all the lawyers to say anything against me.

SCA. You will do as you please, but in your place I would avoid a lawsuit.

ARG. I will never give two hundred pistoles.

SCA. Ah! here is our man.

SCENE IX.--ARGANTE, SCAPIN, SILVESTRE, *dressed out as a bravo*.

SIL. Scapin, show me that Argante who is the father of Octave.

SCA. What for, Sir?

SIL. I have just been told that he wants to go to law with me, and to have my sister's marriage annulled.

SCA. I don't know if such is his intention, but he won't consent to give the two hundred pistoles you asked; he says it's too much.

SIL. S'death! s'blood! If I can but find him, I'll make mince-meat of him, were I to be broken alive on the wheel afterwards.

(ARGANTE *hides, trembling, behind* SCAPIN.)

SCA. Sir, the father of Octave is a brave man, and perhaps he will not be afraid of you.

SIL. Ah! will he not? S'blood! s'death! If he were here, I would in a moment run my sword through his body. (*Seeing* ARGANTE.) Who is that man?

SCA. He's not the man, Sir; he's not the man.

SIL. Is he one of his friends?

SCA. No, Sir; on the contrary, he's his greatest enemy.

SIL. His greatest enemy?

SCA. Yes.

SIL. Ah! zounds! I am delighted at it. (*To* ARGANTE) You are an enemy of that scoundrel Argante, are you?

SCA. Yes, yes; I assure you that it is so.

SIL. (***shaking** ARGANTE'S **hand roughly***). Shake hands, shake hands. I give you my word, I swear upon my honour, by the sword I wear, by all the oaths I can take, that, before the day is over, I shall have delivered you of that rascally knave, of that scoundrel Argante. Trust me.

SCA. But, Sir, violent deeds are not allowed in this country.

SIL. I don't care, and I have nothing to lose.

SCA. He will certainly take his precautions; he has relations, friends, servants, who will take his part against you.

SIL. Blood and thunder! It is all I ask, all I ask. (Drawing his sword.) Ah! s'death! ah! s'blood! Why can I not meet him at this very moment, with all these relations and friends of his? If he would only appear before me, surrounded by a score of them! Why do they not fall upon me, arms in hand? (***Standing upon his guard***.) What! you villains! you dare to attack me? Now, s'death! Kill and slay! (He lunges out on all sides; as if he were fighting many people at once.) No quarter; lay on. Thrust. Firm. Again. Eye and foot. Ah! knaves! ah! rascals! ah! you shall have a taste of it. I'll give you your fill. Come on, you rabble! come on. That's what you want, you there. You shall have your fill of it, I say. Stick to it, you brutes; stick to it. Now, then, parry; now, then, you. (Turning towards ARGANTE and SCAPIN.) Parry this; parry. You draw back? Stand firm, man! S'death! What! Never flinch, I say.

SCA. Sir, we have nothing to do with it.

SIL. That will teach you to trifle with me.

SCENE X.--ARGANTE, SCAPIN.

SCA. Well, Sir, you see how many people are killed for two hundred pistoles. Now I wish you a good morning.

ARG. (*all trembling*). Scapin.

SCA. What do you say?

ARG. I will give the two hundred pistoles.

SCA. I am very glad of it, for your sake.

ARG. Let us go to him; I have them with me.

SCA. Better give them to me. You must not, for your honour, appear in this business, now that you have passed for another; and, besides, I should be afraid that he would ask you for more, if he knew who you are.

ARG. True; still I should be glad to see to whom I give my money.

SCA. Do you mistrust me then?

ARG. Oh no; but....

SCA. Zounds! Sir; either I am a thief or an honest man; one or the other. Do you think I would deceive you, and that in all this I have any other interest at heart than yours and that of my master, whom you want to take into your family? If I have not all your confidence, I will have no more to do with all this, and you can look out for somebody else to get you out of the mess.

ARG. Here then.

SCA. No, Sir; do not trust your money to me. I would rather you trusted another with your message.

ARG. Ah me! here, take it.

SCA. No, no, I tell you; do not trust me. Who knows if I do not want to steal your money from you?

ARG. Take it, I tell you, and don't force me to ask you again. However, mind you have an acknowledgment from him.

SCA. Trust me; he hasn't to do with an idiot.

ARG. I will go home and wait for you.

SCA. I shall be sure to go. (*Alone*.) That one's all right; now for the other. Ah! here he is. They are sent one after the other to fall into my net.

SCENE XI.--GERONTE, SCAPIN.

SCA. (*affecting not to see* GERONTE). O Heaven! O unforeseen misfortune! O unfortunate father! Poor Geronte, what will you do?

GER. (*aside*). What is he saying there with that doleful face?

SCA. Can no one tell me whereto find Mr. Geronte?

GER. What is the matter, Scapin?

SCA. (running about on the stage, and still affecting not to see or hear GERONTE). Where could I meet him, to tell him of this misfortune?

GER. (*stopping* SCAPIN). What is the matter?

SCA. (*as before*). In vain I run everywhere to meet him. I cannot find him.

GER. Here I am.

SCA. (*as before*). He must have hidden himself in some place which nobody can guess.

GER. (*stopping* SCAPIN *again*). Ho! I say, are you blind? Can't you see me?

SCA. Ah! Sir, it is impossible to find you.

GER. I have been near you for the last half-hour. What is it all about?

SCA. Sir....

GER. Well!

SCA. Your son, Sir....

GER. Well! My son....

SCA. Has met with the strangest misfortune you ever heard of.

GER. What is it?

SCA. This afternoon I found him looking very sad about something which you had said to him, and in which you had very improperly mixed my name. While trying: to dissipate his sorrow, we went and walked about in the harbour. There, among other things, was to be seen a Turkish galley. A young Turk, with a gentlemanly look about him, invited us to go in, and held out his hand to us. We went in. He was most civil to us; gave us some lunch, with the most excellent fruit and the best wine you have ever seen.

GER. What is there so sad about all this?

SCA. Wait a little; it is coming. Whilst we were eating, the galley left the harbour, and when in the open sea, the Turk made me go down into a boat, and sent me to tell you that unless you sent by me five hundred crowns, he would take your son prisoner to Algiers.

GER. What! five hundred crowns!

SCA. Yes, Sir; and, moreover, he only gave me two hours to find them in.

GER. Ah! the scoundrel of a Turk to murder me in that fashion!

SCA. It is for you, Sir, to see quickly about the means of saving from slavery a son whom you love so tenderly.

GER. What the deuce did he want to go in that galley for? [Footnote: ***Que diable allait-il faire dans cette galere?*** This sentence has become established in the language with the meaning, "Whatever business had he there?"]

SCA. He had no idea of what would happen.

GER. Go, Scapin, go quickly, and tell that Turk that I shall send the police after him.

SCA. The police in the open sea! Are you joking?

GER. What the deuce did he want to go in that galley for?

SCA. A cruel destiny will sometimes lead people.

GER. Listen, Scapin; you must act in this the part of a faithful servant.

SCA. How, Sir?

GER. You must go and tell that Turk that he must send me back my son, and that you will take his place until I have found the sum he asks.

SCA. Ah! Sir; do you know what you are saying? and do you fancy that that Turk will be foolish enough to receive a poor wretch like me in your son's stead?

The Impostures of Scapin

GER. What the deuce did he want to go in that galley for?

SCA. He could not foresee his misfortune. However, Sir, remember that he has given me only two hours.

GER. You say that he asks....

SCA. Five hundred crowns.

GER. Five hundred crowns! Has he no conscience?

SCA. Ah! ah! Conscience in a Turk!

GER. Does he understand what five hundred crowns are?

SCA. Yes, Sir, he knows that five hundred crowns are one thousand five hundred francs. [Footnote: The *ecu* stands usually for *petit ecu*, which equalled three franks. "Crown," employed in a general sense, seems the only translation possible.]

GER. Does the scoundrel think that one thousand five hundred francs are to be found in the gutter?

SCA. Such people will never listen to reason.

GER. But what the deuce did he want to go in that galley for?

SCA. Ah! what a waste of words! Leave the galley alone; remember that time presses, and that you are running the risk of losing your son for ever. Alas! my poor master, perhaps I shall never see you again, and that at this very moment, whilst I am speaking to you, they are taking you away to make a slave of you in Algiers! But Heaven is my witness that I did all I could, and that, if you are not brought back, it is all owing to the want of love of your father.

GER. Wait a minute, Scapin; I will go and fetch that sum of money.

SCA. Be quick, then, for I am afraid of not being in time.

GER. You said four hundred crowns; did you not?

SCA. No, five hundred crowns.

GER. Five hundred crowns!

SCA. Yes.

GER. What the deuce did he want to go in that galley for?

SCA. Quite right, but be quick.

GER. Could he not have chosen another walk?

SCA. It is true; but act promptly.

GER. Cursed galley!

SCA. (*aside*) That galley sticks in his throat.

GER. Here, Scapin; I had forgotten that I have just received this sum in gold, and I had no idea it would so soon be wrenched from me. (Taking his purse out of his pocket, and making as if he were giving it to SCAPIN.) But mind you tell that Turk that he is a scoundrel.

SCA. (*holding out his hand*). Yes.

GER. (*as above*). An infamous wretch.

SCA. (*still holding out his hand*). Yes.

GER. (*as above*). A man without conscience, a thief.

SCA. Leave that to me.

GER. (*as above*). That....

SCA. All right.

GER. (*as above*). And that, if ever I catch him, he will pay for it.

SCA. Yes.

GER. (*putting back the purse in his pocket*). Go, go quickly, and fetch my son.

SCA. (*running after him*). Hallo! Sir.

GER. Well?

SCA. And the money?

GER. Did I not give it to you?

SCA. No, indeed, you put it back in pour pocket.

GER. Ah! it is grief which troubles my mind.

SCA. So I see.

GER. What the deuce did he want to go in that galley for? Ah! cursed galley! Scoundrel of a Turk! May the devil take you!

SCAPIN (*alone*). He can't get over the five hundred crowns I wrench from him; but he has not yet done with me, and I will make him pay in a different money his imposture about me to his son.

SCENE XII.-OCTAVE, LEANDRE, SCAPIN.

OCT. Well, Scapin, have your plans been successful?

LEA. Have you done anything towards alleviating my sorrow?

SCA. (*to* OCTAVE). Here are two hundred pistoles I have got from your father.

OCT. Ah! how happy you make me.

SCA. (*to* LEANDRE), But I could do nothing for you.

LEA. (*going away*). Then I must die, Sir, for I could not live without Zerbinette.

SCA. Hallo! stop, stop; my goodness, how quick you are!

LEA. What can become of me?

SCA. There, there, I have all you want.

LEA. Ah! you bring me back to life again.

SCA. But I give it you only on one condition, which is that you will allow me to revenge myself a little on your father for the trick he has played me.

LEA. You may do as you please.

SCA. You promise it to me before witnesses?

LEA. Yes.

SCA. There, take these five hundred crowns.

LEA. Ah! I will go at once and buy her whom I adore.

ACT III.

SCENE I.--ZERBINETTE, HYACINTHA, SCAPIN, SILVESTRE.

SIL. Yes; your lovers have decided that you should be together, and we are acting according to their orders.

HYA. (*to* ZERBINETTE). Such an order has nothing in it but what is pleasant to me. I receive such a companion with joy, and it will not be my fault if the friendship which exists between those we love does not exist also between us two.

ZER. I accept the offer, and I am not one to draw back when friendship is asked of me.

SCA. And when it is love that is asked of you?

ZER. Ah! love is a different thing. One runs more risk, and I feel less determined.

SCA. You are determined enough against my master, and yet what he has just done for you ought to give you confidence enough to respond to his love as you should.

ZER. As yet I only half trust him, and what he has just done is not sufficient to reassure me. I am of a happy disposition, and am very fond of fun, it is true. But though I laugh, I am serious about many things; and your master will find himself deceived if he thinks that it is sufficient for him to have bought me, for me to be altogether his. He will have to give something else besides money, and for me to answer to his love as he wishes me, he must give me his word, with an accompaniment of certain little ceremonies which are thought indispensable.

SCA. It is so he understands this matter. He only wants you as his wife, and I am not a man to have mixed in this business if he had meant anything else.

ZER. I believe it since you say so; but I foresee certain difficulties with the father.

SCA. We shall find a way of settling that.

HYA. (*to* ZERBINETTE). The similarity of our fate ought to

strengthen the tie of friendship between us. We are both subject to the same fears, both exposed to the same misfortune.

ZER. You have this advantage at least that you know who your parents are, and that, sure of their help, when you wish to make them known, you can secure your happiness by obtaining a consent to the marriage you have contracted. But I, on the contrary, have no such hope to fall back upon, and the position I am in is little calculated to satisfy the wishes of a father whose whole care is money.

HYA. That is true; but you have this in your favour, that the one you love is under no temptation of contracting another marriage.

ZER. A change in a lover's heart is not what we should fear the most. We may justly rely on our own power to keep the conquest we have made; but what I particularly dread is the power of the fathers; for we cannot expect to see them moved by our merit.

HYA. Alas! Why must the course of true love never run smooth? How sweet it would be to love with no link wanting in those chains which unite two hearts.

SCA. How mistaken you are about this! Security in love forms a very unpleasant calm. Constant happiness becomes wearisome. We want ups and downs in life; and the difficulties which generally beset our path in this world revive us, and increase our sense of pleasure.

ZER. Do tell us, Scapin, all about that stratagem of yours, which, I was told, is so very amusing; and how you managed to get some money out of your old miser. You know that the trouble of telling me something amusing is not lost upon me, and that I well repay those who take that trouble by the pleasure it gives me.

SCA. Silvestre here will do that as well as I. I am nursing in my heart a certain little scheme of revenge which I mean to enjoy thoroughly.

SIL. Why do you recklessly engage in enterprises that may bring you into trouble?

SCA. I delight in dangerous enterprises.

SIL. As I told you already, you would give up the idea you have if you would listen to me.

SCA. I prefer listening to myself.

SIL. Why the deuce do you engage in such a business?

SCA. Why the deuce do you trouble yourself about it?

SIL. It is because I can see that you will without necessity bring a storm of blows upon yourself.

SCA. Ah, well, it will be on my shoulders, and not on yours.

SIL. It is true that you are master of your own shoulders, and at liberty to dispose of them as you please.

SCA. Such dangers never stop me, and I hate those fearful hearts which, by dint of thinking of what may happen, never undertake anything.

ZER. (*to* SCAPIN). But we shall want you.

SCA. Oh, yes! but I shall soon be with you again. It shall never be said that a man has with impunity put me into a position of betraying myself, and of revealing secrets which it were better should not be known.

SCENE II.--GERONTE, SCAPIN.

GER. Well! Scapin, and how have we succeeded about my son's mischance?

SCA. Your son is safe, Sir; but you now run the greatest danger imaginable, and I sincerely wish you were safe in your house.

GER. How is that?

SCA. While I am speaking to you, there are people who are looking out for you everywhere.

GER. For me?

SCA. Yes.

GER. But who?

SCA. The brother of that young girl whom Octave has married. He thinks that you are trying to break off that match, because you intend to give to your daughter the place she occupies in the heart of Octave; and he has resolved to wreak his vengeance upon you. All his friends, men of the sword like himself, are looking out for you, and are seeking you everywhere. I have met with scores here and there, soldiers of his company, who question every one they meet, and occupy in companies all the thoroughfares leading to your house, so that you cannot go home either to the right or the left without falling into their hands.

GER. What can I do, my dear Scapin?

SCA. I am sure I don't know, Sir; it is an unpleasant business. I tremble for you from head to foot and.... Wait a moment.

(SCAPIN goes to see in the back of the stage if there is anybody coming.)

GER. (*trembling*). Well?

SCA. (*coming back*). No, no; 'tis nothing.

GER. Could you not find out some means of saving me?

SCA. I can indeed think of one, but I should run the risk of a sound beating.

GER. Ah! Scapin, show yourself a devoted servant. Do not forsake me, I pray you.

SCA. I will do what I can. I feel for you a tenderness which renders it impossible for me to leave you without help.

GER. Be sure that I will reward you for it, Scapin, and I promise you this coat of mine when it is a little more worn.

SCA. Wait a minute. I have just thought, at the proper moment, of the very thing to save you. You must get into this sack, and I....

GER. (*thinking he sees somebody*). Ah!

SCA. No, no, no, no; 'tis nobody. As I was saying, you must get in here, and must be very careful not to stir. I will put you on my shoulders, and carry you like a bundle of something or other. I shall thus be able to take you through your enemies, and see you safe into your house. When there, we will barricade the door and send for help.

GER. A very good idea.

SCA. The best possible. You will see. (*Aside*) Ah! you shall pay me for that lie.

GER. What?

SCA. I only say that your enemies will be finely caught. Get in right to the bottom, and, above all things, be careful not to show yourself and not to move, whatever may happen.

GER. You may trust me to keep still.

SCA. Hide yourself; here comes one of the bullies! He is looking for you. (*Altering his voice*.) [Footnote: All the parts within inverted commas are supposed to be spoken by the man Scapin is personating; the rest by himself.] "Vat! I shall not hab de pleasure to kill dis Geronte, and one vill not in sharity show me vere is he?" (*To* GERONTE, *in his ordinary tone*) Do not stir. "Pardi! I vill find him if he lied in de mittle ob de eart" (*To* GERONTE, *in his natural tone*) Do not show yourself. "Ho! you man vid a sack!" Sir! "I will give thee a pound if thou vilt tell me where dis Geronte is." You are looking for Mr. Geronte? "Yes, dat I am." And on what business, Sir? "For vat pusiness?"

Yes. "I vill, pardi! trash him vid one stick to dead." Oh! Sir, people like him are not thrashed with sticks, and he is not a man to be treated so. "Vat! dis fob of a Geronte, dis prute, dis cat." Mr. Geronte, Sir, is neither a fop, a brute, nor a cad; and you ought, if you please, to speak differently. "Vat! you speak so mighty vit me?" I am defending, as I ought, an honourable man who is maligned. "Are you one friend of dis Geronte?" Yes, Sir, I am. "Ah, ah! You are one friend of him, dat is goot luck!" (Beating the sack several times with the stick.) "Here is vat I give you for him." (Calling out as if he received the beating) Ah! ah! ah! ah! Sir. Ah! ah! Sir, gently! Ah! pray. Ah! ah! ah! "Dere, bear him dat from me. Goot-pye." Ah! the wretch. Ah!...ah!

GER. (*looking out*). Ah! Scapin, I can bear it no longer.

SCA. Ah! Sir, I am bruised all over, and my shoulders are as sore as can be.

GER. How! It was on mine he laid his stick.

SCA. I beg your pardon, Sir, it was on my back.

GER. What do you mean? I am sure I felt the blows, and feel them still.

SCA. No, I tell you; it was only the end of his stick that reached your shoulders.

GER. You should have gone a little farther back, then, to spare me, and....

SCA. (*pushing* GERONTE'S *head back into the sack*). Take care, here is another man who looks like a foreigner. "Frient, me run like one Dutchman, and me not fint all de tay dis treatful Geronte." Hide yourself well. "Tell me, you, Sir gentleman, if you please, know you not vere is dis Geronte, vat me look for?" No, Sir, I do not know where Geronte is. "Tell me, trutful, me not vant much vit him. Only to gife him one tosen plows vid a stick, and two or tree runs vid a swort tro' his shest." I assure you, Sir, I do not know where he is. "It seems me I see sometink shake in dat sack." Excuse me, Sir. "I pe shure dere is sometink or oder in dat sack." Not at all, Sir. "Me should like to gife one plow of de swort in dat sack." Ah! Sir, beware, pray you, of doing so. "Put, show me ten vat to be dere?" Gently, Sir. "Why chently?" You have nothing to do with what I am carrying. "And I, put I vill see." You shall not see. "Ah! vat trifling." It is some clothes of mine. "Show me tem, I tell you." I will not. "You vill not?" No. "I make you feel this shtick upon de sholders." I don't care. "Ah! you vill poast!" (Striking the sack, and calling out as if he were beaten) Oh! oh! oh! Oh! Sir. Oh! oh! "Goot-bye, dat is one littel lesson teach you to speak so insolent." Ah! plague the crazy jabberer! Oh!

GER. (*looking out of the sack*). Ah! all my bones are broken.

SCA. Ah! I am dying.

GER. Why the deuce do they strike on my back?

SCA. (*pushing his head back into the bag*). Take care; I see half a dozen soldiers coming together. (Imitating the voices of several people.) "Now, we must discover Geronte; let us look everywhere carefully. We must spare no trouble, scour the town, and not forget one single spot Let us search on all sides. Which way shall we go? Let us go that way. No, this. On the left. On the right. No; yes." (*To* GERONTE *in his ordinary voice*) Hide yourself well. "Ah! here is his servant. I say, you rascal, you must tell us where your master is. Speak. Be quick. At once. Make haste. Now." Ah! gentlemen, one moment. (GERONTE looks quietly out of the bag, and sees **SCAPIN'S** trick.) "If you do not tell us at once where your master is, we will shower a rain of blows on your back." I had rather suffer anything than tell you where my master is. "Very well, we will cudgel you soundly." Do as you please. "You want to be beaten, then?" I will never betray my master. "Ah! you will have it--there." Oh!

(*As he is going to strike*, GERONTE gets out of the bag, and **SCAPIN** runs away.)

GER. (*alone*). Ah! infamous wretch! ah I rascal! ah! scoundrel! It is thus that you murder me?

SCENE III.--ZERBINETTE, GERONTE.

ZER. (*laughing, without seeing* GERONTE). Ah, ah! I must really come and breathe a little.

GER. (*aside, not seeing* ZERBINETTE). Ah! I will make you pay for it.

ZER. (*not seeing* GERONTE). Ah, ah, ah, ah! What an amusing story! What a good dupe that old man is!

GER. This is no matter for laughter; and you have no business to laugh at it.

ZER. Why? What do you mean, Sir?

The Impostures of Scapin

GER. I mean to say that you ought not to laugh at me.

ZER. Laugh at you?

GER. Yes.

ZER. How! Who is thinking of laughing at you?

GER. Why do you come and laugh in my face?

ZER. This has nothing to do with you. I am only laughing with myself at the remembrance of a story which has just been told me. The most amusing story in the world. I don't know if it is because I am interested in the matter, but I never heard anything so absurd as the trick that has just been played by a son to his father to get some money out of him.

GER. By a son to his father to get some money out of him?

ZER. Yes; and if you are at all desirous of hearing how it was done, I will tell you the whole affair. I have a natural longing for imparting to others the funny things I know.

GER. Pray, tell me that story.

ZER. Willingly. I shall not risk much by telling it you, for it is an adventure which is not likely to remain secret long. Fate placed me among one of those bands of people who are called gypsies, and who, tramping from province to province, tell you your fortune, and do many other things besides. When we came to this town, I met a young man, who, on seeing me, fell in love with me. From that moment he followed me everywhere; and, like all young men, he imagined that he had but to speak and things would go on as he liked; but he met with a pride which forced him to think twice. He spoke of his love to the people in whose power I was, and found them ready to give me up for a certain sum of money. But the sad part of the business was that my lover found himself exactly in the same condition as most young men of good family, that is, without any money at all. His father, although rich, is the veriest old skinflint and greatest miser you ever heard of. Wait a moment--what is his name? I don't remember it--can't you help me? Can't you name some one in this town who is known to be the most hard-fisted old miser in the place?

GER. No.

ZER. There is in his name some Ron...Ronte... Or...Oronte...No. Ge...Geronte. Yes, Geronte, that's my miser's name. I have it now; it is the old churl I mean. Well, to come back to our story. Our people wished to leave this town to-day, and my lover would have lost me through his lack of money if, in order to wrench some out of his father, he had not made use of a clever servant he has. As for that servant's name, I remember it very well. His name is Scapin. He is a most wonderful man, and deserves the highest praise.

GER. (*aside*). Ah, the wretch!

ZER. But just listen to the plan he adopted to take in his dupe--ah! ah! ah! I can't think of it without laughing heartily--ah! ah! ah! He went to that old screw--ah! ah! ah!--and told him that while he was walking about the harbour with his son--ah! ah!--they noticed a Turkish galley; that a young Turk had invited them to come in and see it; that he had given them some lunch--ah! ah!--and that, while they were at table, the galley had gone into the open sea; that the Turk had sent him alone back, with the express order to say to him that, unless he sent him five hundred crowns, he would take his son to be a slave in Algiers--ah, ah, ah! You may imagine our miser, our stingy old curmudgeon, in the greatest anguish, struggling between his love for his son and his love for his money. Those five hundred crowns that are asked of him are five hundred dagger-thrusts--ah! ah! ah! ah! He can't bring his mind to tear out, as it were, this sum from his heart, and his anguish makes him think of the most ridiculous means to find money for his son's ransom--ah! ah! ah! He wants to send the police into the open sea after the Turk's galley--ah! ah! ah! He asks his servant to take the place of his son till he has found the money to pay for him--money he has no intention of giving--ah! ah! ah! He yields up, to make the five hundred crowns, three or four old suits which are not worth thirty--ah! ah! ah! The servant shows him each time how absurd is what he proposes, and each reflection of the old fellow is accompanied by an agonising, "But what the deuce did he want to go in that galley for? Ah! cursed galley. Ah! scoundrel of a Turk!" At last, after many hesitations, after having sighed and groaned for a long time...But it seems to me that my story does not make you laugh; what do you say to it?

GER. What I say? That the young man is a scoundrel--a good-for-nothing fellow--who will be punished by his father for the trick he has played him; that the gypsy girl is a bold, impudent hussy to come and insult a man of honour, who will give her what she deserves for coming here to debauch the sons of good families; and that the servant is an infamous wretch, whom Geronte will take care to have hung before to-morrow is over.

SCENE IV.--ZERBINETTE, SILVESTRE.

SIL. Where are you running away to? Do you know that the man you were speaking to is your lover's father?

ZER. I have just begun to suspect that it was so; and I related to him his own story without knowing who he was.

SIL. What do you mean by his story?

ZER. Yes; I was so full of that story that I longed to tell it to somebody. But what does it matter? So much the worse for him. I do not see that things can be made either better or worse.

SIL. You must have been in a great hurry to chatter; and it is indiscretion, indeed, not to keep silent on your own affairs.

ZER. Oh! he would have heard it from somebody else.

SCENE V.--ARGANTE, ZERBINETTE, SILVESTRE.

ARG. (**behind the scenes**). Hullo! Silvestre.

SIL. (**to** ZERBINETTE). Go in there; my master is calling me.

SCENE VI.--ARGANTE, SILVESTRE.

ARG. So you agreed, you rascals; you agreed--Scapin, you, and my son --to cheat me out of my money; and you think that I am going to bear it patiently?

SIL. Upon my word, Sir, if Scapin is deceiving you, it is none of my doing. I assure you that I have nothing whatever to do with it.

ARG. We shall see, you rascal! we shall see; and I am not going to be made a fool of for nothing.

SCENE VII.-GERONTE, ARGANTE, SILVESTRE.

GER. Ah! Mr. Argante, you see me in the greatest trouble.

ARG. And I am in the greatest sorrow.

GER. This rascal, Scapin, has got five hundred crowns out of me.

ARG. Yes, and this same rascal, Scapin, two hundred pistoles out of me.

GER. He was not satisfied with getting those five hundred crowns, but treated me besides in a manner I am ashamed to speak of. But he--shall pay me for it.

ARG. I shall have him punished for the trick he has played me.

GER. And I mean to make an example of him.

SIL. (*aside*). May Heaven grant that I do not catch my share of all this!

GER. But, Mr. Argante, this is not all; and misfortunes, as you know, never come alone. I was looking forward to the happiness of to-day seeing my daughter, who was everything to me; and I have just heard that she left Tarentum a long while since; and there is every reason to suppose that the ship was wrecked, and that she is lost to me for ever.

ARG. But why did you keep her in Tarentum, instead of enjoying the happiness of having her with you?

GER. I had my reasons for it; some family interests forced me till now to keep my second marriage secret. But what do I see?

SCENE VIII.--ARGANTE, GERONTE, NERINE, SILVESTRE.

GER. What! you here, Nerine?

NER. (*on her knees before* GERONTE). Ah! Mr. Pandolphe, how....

GER. Call me Geronte, and do not use the other name any more. The reasons which forced me to take it at Tarentum exist no longer.

NER. Alas! what sorrow that change of name has caused us; what troubles and difficulties in trying to find you out!

GER. And where are my daughter and her mother?

NER. Your daughter, Sir, is not far from here; but before I go to fetch her, I must ask you to forgive me for having married her, because of the forsaken state we found ourselves in, when we had no longer any hope of meeting you.

GER. My daughter is married?

NER. Yes, Sir.

GER. And to whom?

NER. To a young man, called Octave, the son of a certain Mr. Argante.

GER. O Heaven!

ARG. What an extraordinary coincidence.

GER. Take us quickly where she is.

NER. You have but to come into this house.

GER. Go in first; follow me, follow me, Mr. Argante.

SIL. (alone). Well, this is a strange affair.

SCENE IX.--SCAPIN, SILVESTRE.

SCA. Well, Silvestre, what are our people doing?

SIL. I have two things to tell you. One is that Octave is all right; our Hyacintha is, it seems, the daughter of Geronte, and chance has brought to pass what the wisdom of the fathers had decided. The other, that the old men threaten you with the greatest punishments-- particularly Mr. Geronte.

SCA. Oh, that's nothing. Threats have never done me any harm as yet; they are but clouds which pass away far above our heads.

SIL. You had better take care. The sons may get reconciled to their fathers, and leave you in the lurch.

SCA. Leave that to me. I shall find the means of soothing their anger, and....

SIL. Go away; I see them coming.

SCENE X.--GERONTE, ARGANTE, HYACINTHA, ZERBINETTE, NERINE, SILVESTRE.

GER. Come, my daughter; come to my house. My happiness would be perfect if your mother had been with you.

ARG. Here is Octave coming just at the right time.

SCENE XI.--ARGANTE, GERONTE, OCTAVE, HYACINTHA, ZERBINETTE, NERINE,
SILVESTRE.

ARG. Come, my son, come and rejoice with us about the happiness of your marriage. Heaven....

OCT. No, father, all your proposals for marriage are useless. I must be open with you, and you have been told how I am engaged.

ARG. Yes; but what you do not know....

OCT. I know all I care to know.

ARG. I mean to say that the daughter of Mr. Geronte....

OCT. The daughter of Mr. Geronte will never be anything to me.

GER. It is she who....

OCT. (*to* GERONTE). You need not go on, Sir; I hope you will forgive me, but I shall abide by my resolution.

SIL. (*to* OCTAVE). Listen....

OCT. Be silent; I will listen to nothing.

ARG. (*to* OCTAVE). Your wife....

OCT. No, father, I would rather die than lose my dear Hyacintha (***crossing the theatre, and placing himself by*** HYACINTHA). Yes, all you would do is useless; this is the one to whom my heart is engaged. I will have no other wife.

ARG. Well! she it is whom we give you. What a madcap you are never to listen to anything but your own foolish whim.

HYA. (***showing*** GERONTE). Yes, Octave, this is my father whom I have found again, and all our troubles are over.

GER. Let us go home; we shall talk more comfortably at home.

HYA. (*showing* ZERBINETTE). Ah! father, I beg of you the favour not to part me from this charming young lady. She has noble qualities, which will be sure to make you like her when you know her.

GER. What! do you wish me to take to my house a girl with whom your brother is in love, and who told me to my face so many insulting things?

ZER. Pray forgive me, Sir; I should not have spoken in that way if I had known who you were, and I only knew you by reputation.

GER. By reputation; what do you mean?

HYA. Father, I can answer for it that she is most virtuous, and that the love my brother has for her is pure.

GER. It is all very well. You would try now to persuade me to marry my son to her, a stranger, a street-girl!

SCENE XII.-ARGANTE, GERONTE, LEANDRE, OCTAVE, HYACINTHA, ZERBINETTE,
NERINE, SILVESTRE.

LEA. My father, you must no longer say that I love a stranger without birth or wealth. Those from whom I bought her have just told me that she belongs to an honest family in this town. They stole her away when she was four years old, and here is a bracelet which they gave me, and which will help me to discover her family.

ARG. Ah! To judge by this bracelet, this is my daughter whom I lost when she was four years old.

GER. Your daughter?

ARG. Yes, I see she is my daughter. I know all her features again. My dear child!

GER. Oh! what wonderful events!

SCENE XIII.--ARGANTE, GERONTE, LEANDRE, OCTAVE, HYACINTHA, ZERBINETTE, NERINE, SILVESTRE, CARLE.

CAR. Ah! gentlemen, a most sad accident has just taken place.

GER. What is it?

CAR. Poor Scapin....

GER. Is a rascal whom I shall see hung.

CAR. Alas! Sir, you will not have that trouble. As he was passing near a building, a bricklayer's hammer fell on his head and broke his skull, leaving his brain exposed. He is dying, and he has asked to be brought in here to speak to you before he dies.

SCENE XIV.--ARGANTE, GERONTE, LEANDRE, OCTAVE, HYACINTHA, ZERBINETTE,
NERINE. SILVESTRE, CARLE, SCAPIN.

SCA. (brought in by some men, his head wrapped up, as if he were wounded). Oh, oh! gentlemen, you see me.... Oh! You see me in a sad state. Oh! I would not die without coming to ask forgiveness of all those I may have offended. Oh! Yes, gentlemen, before I give up the ghost, I beseech you to forgive me all I have done amiss, and particularly Mr. Argante and Mr. Geronte. Oh!

ARG. I forgive you; die in peace, Scapin.

SCA. (*to* GERONTE). It is you, Sir, I have offended the most, because of the beating with the cudgel which I....

GER. Leave that alone.

SCA. I feel in dying an inconceivable grief for the beating which I....

GER. Ah me! be silent.

SCA. That unfortunate beating that I gave....

GER. Be silent, I tell you; I forgive you everything.

SCA. Alas! how good you are. But is it really with all your heart that you forgive me the beating which I...?

GER. Yes, yes; don't mention it. I forgive you everything. You are punished.

SCA. Ah! Sir, how much better I feel for your kind words.

GER. Yes, I forgive you; but on one condition, that you die.

SCA. How! Sir?

GER. I retract my words if you recover.

SCA. Oh! oh! all my pains are coming hack.

ARG. Mr. Geronte, let us forgive him without any condition, for we are all so happy.

GER. Well, be it so.

ARG. Let us go to supper, and talk of our happiness.

SCA. And you, take me to the end of the table; it is there I will await death.

www.bookjungle.com *email: sales@bookjungle.com fax: 630-214-0564 mail: Book Jungle PO Box 2226 Champaign, IL 61825*

The Codes Of Hammurabi And Moses
W. W. Davies

QTY

The discovery of the Hammurabi Code is one of the greatest achievements of archaeology, and is of paramount interest, not only to the student of the Bible, but also to all those interested in ancient history...

Religion   **ISBN:** *1-59462-338-4*   **Pages:**132
MSRP $12.95

The Theory of Moral Sentiments
Adam Smith

QTY

This work from 1749. contains original theories of conscience amd moral judgment and it is the foundation for systemof morals.

Philosophy   **ISBN:** *1-59462-777-0*   **Pages:**536
MSRP $19.95

Jessica's First Prayer
Hesba Stretton

QTY

In a screened and secluded corner of one of the many railway-bridges which span the streets of London there could be seen a few years ago, from five o'clock every morning until half past eight, a tidily set-out coffee-stall, consisting of a trestle and board, upon which stood two large tin cans, with a small fire of charcoal burning under each so as to keep the coffee boiling during the early hours of the morning when the work-people were thronging into the city on their way to their daily toil...

Childrens   **ISBN:** *1-59462-373-2*   **Pages:**84
MSRP $9.95

My Life and Work
Henry Ford

QTY

Henry Ford revolutionized the world with his implementation of mass production for the Model T automobile. Gain valuable business insight into his life and work with his own auto-biography... "We have only started on our development of our country we have not as yet, with all our talk of wonderful progress, done more than scratch the surface. The progress has been wonderful enough but..."

Biographies/   **ISBN:** *1-59462-198-5*   **Pages:**300
MSRP $21.95

www.bookjungle.com *email: sales@bookjungle.com fax: 630-214-0564 mail: Book Jungle PO Box 2226 Champaign, IL 61825*

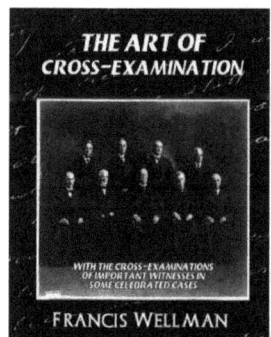

The Art of Cross-Examination
Francis Wellman

QTY

I presume it is the experience of every author, after his first book is published upon an important subject, to be almost overwhelmed with a wealth of ideas and illustrations which could readily have been included in his book, and which to his own mind, at least, seem to make a second edition inevitable. Such certainly was the case with me; and when the first edition had reached its sixth impression in five months, I rejoiced to learn that it seemed to my publishers that the book had met with a sufficiently favorable reception to justify a second and considerably enlarged edition. ..

Reference   ISBN: *1-59462-647-2*   **Pages:412**   *MSRP $19.95*

On the Duty of Civil Disobedience
Henry David Thoreau

QTY

Thoreau wrote his famous essay, On the Duty of Civil Disobedience, as a protest against an unjust but popular war and the immoral but popular institution of slave-owning. He did more than write—he declined to pay his taxes, and was hauled off to gaol in consequence. Who can say how much this refusal of his hastened the end of the war and of slavery ?

Law   ISBN: *1-59462-747-9*   **Pages:48**   *MSRP $7.45*

Dream Psychology Psychoanalysis for Beginners
Sigmund Freud

QTY

Sigmund Freud, born Sigismund Schlomo Freud (May 6, 1856 - September 23, 1939), was a Jewish-Austrian neurologist and psychiatrist who co-founded the psychoanalytic school of psychology. Freud is best known for his theories of the unconscious mind, especially involving the mechanism of repression; his redefinition of sexual desire as mobile and directed towards a wide variety of objects; and his therapeutic techniques, especially his understanding of transference in the therapeutic relationship and the presumed value of dreams as sources of insight into unconscious desires.

Psychology   ISBN: *1-59462-905-6*   **Pages:196**   *MSRP $15.45*

The Miracle of Right Thought
Orison Swett Marden

QTY

Believe with all of your heart that you will do what you were made to do. When the mind has once formed the habit of holding cheerful, happy, prosperous pictures, it will not be easy to form the opposite habit. It does not matter how improbable or how far away this realization may see, or how dark the prospects may be, if we visualize them as best we can, as vividly as possible, hold tenaciously to them and vigorously struggle to attain them, they will gradually become actualized, realized in the life. But a desire, a longing without endeavor, a yearning abandoned or held indifferently will vanish without realization.

Self Help   ISBN: *1-59462-644-8*   **Pages:360**   *MSRP $25.45*

www.bookjungle.com *email: sales@bookjungle.com fax: 630-214-0564 mail: Book Jungle PO Box 2226 Champaign, IL 61825*

QTY

	Title	ISBN	Price
☐	**The Rosicrucian Cosmo-Conception Mystic Christianity** by *Max Heindel*	ISBN: 1-59462-188-8	**$38.95**

The Rosicrucian Cosmo-conception is not dogmatic, neither does it appeal to any other authority than the reason of the student. It is; not controversial, but is: sent forth in the, hope that it may help to clear... New Age/Religion Pages 646

☐ **Abandonment To Divine Providence** by *Jean-Pierre de Caussade*   ISBN: 1-59462-228-0   **$25.95**
"The Rev. Jean Pierre de Caussade was one of the most remarkable spiritual writers of the Society of Jesus in France in the 18th Century. His death took place at Toulouse in 1751. His works have gone through many editions and have been republished...   Inspirational/Religion Pages 400

☐ **Mental Chemistry** by *Charles Haanel*   ISBN: 1-59462-192-6   **$23.95**
Mental Chemistry allows the change of material conditions by combining and appropriately utilizing the power of the mind. Much like applied chemistry creates something new and unique out of careful combinations of chemicals the mastery of mental chemistry...   New Age Pages 354

☐ **The Letters of Robert Browning and Elizabeth Barret Barrett 1845-1846 vol II**   ISBN: 1-59462-193-4   **$35.95**
by *Robert Browning* and *Elizabeth Barrett*   Biographies Pages 596

☐ **Gleanings In Genesis (volume I)** by *Arthur W. Pink*   ISBN: 1-59462-130-6   **$27.45**
Appropriately has Genesis been termed "the seed plot of the Bible" for in it we have, in germ form, almost all of the great doctrines which are afterwards fully developed in the books of Scripture which follow...   Religion/Inspirational Pages 420

☐ **The Master Key** by *L. W. de Laurence*   ISBN: 1-59462-001-6   **$30.95**
In no branch of human knowledge has there been a more lively increase of the spirit of research during the past few years than in the study of Psychology, Concentration and Mental Discipline. The requests for authentic lessons in Thought Control, Mental Discipline and...   New Age/Business Pages 422

☐ **The Lesser Key Of Solomon Goetia** by *L. W. de Laurence*   ISBN: 1-59462-092-X   **$9.95**
This translation of the first book of the "Lernegton" which is now for the first time made accessible to students of Talismanic Magic was done, after careful collation and edition, from numerous Ancient Manuscripts in Hebrew, Latin, and French...   New Age/Occult Pages 92

☐ **Rubaiyat Of Omar Khayyam** by *Edward Fitzgerald*   ISBN:1-59462-332-5   **$13.95**
Edward Fitzgerald, whom the world has already learned, in spite of his own efforts to remain within the shadow of anonymity, to look upon as one of the rarest poets of the century, was born at Bredfield, in Suffolk, on the 31st of March, 1809. He was the third son of John Purcell...   Music Pages 172

☐ **Ancient Law** by *Henry Maine*   ISBN: 1-59462-128-4   **$29.95**
The chief object of the following pages is to indicate some of the earliest ideas of mankind, as they are reflected in Ancient Law, and to point out the relation of those ideas to modern thought.   Religion/History Pages 452

☐ **Far-Away Stories** by *William J. Locke*   ISBN: 1-59462-129-2   **$19.45**
"Good wine needs no bush, but a collection of mixed vintages does. And this book is just such a collection. Some of the stories I do not want to remain buried for ever in the museum files of dead magazine-numbers an author's not unpardonable vanity..."   Fiction Pages 272

☐ **Life of David Crockett** by *David Crockett*   ISBN: 1-59462-250-7   **$27.45**
"Colonel David Crockett was one of the most remarkable men of the times in which he lived. Born in humble life, but gifted with a strong will, an indomitable courage, and unremitting perseverance...   Biographies/New Age Pages 424

☐ **Lip-Reading** by *Edward Nitchie*   ISBN: 1-59462-206-X   **$25.95**
Edward B. Nitchie, founder of the New York School for the Hard of Hearing, now the Nitchie School of Lip-Reading, Inc, wrote "LIP-READING Principles and Practice". The development and perfecting of this meritorious work on lip-reading was an undertaking...   How-to Pages 400

☐ **A Handbook of Suggestive Therapeutics, Applied Hypnotism, Psychic Science**   ISBN: 1-59462-214-0   **$24.95**
by *Henry Munro*   Health/New Age/Health/Self-help Pages 376

☐ **A Doll's House: and Two Other Plays** by *Henrik Ibsen*   ISBN: 1-59462-112-8   **$19.95**
Henrik Ibsen created this classic when in revolutionary 1848 Rome. Introducing some striking concepts in playwriting for the realist genre, this play has been studied the world over.   Fiction/Classics/Plays 308

☐ **The Light of Asia** by *sir Edwin Arnold*   ISBN: 1-59462-204-3   **$13.95**
In this poetic masterpiece, Edwin Arnold describes the life and teachings of Buddha. The man who was to become known as Buddha to the world was born as Prince Gautama of India but he rejected the worldly riches and abandoned the reigns of power when...   Religion/History/Biographies Pages 170

☐ **The Complete Works of Guy de Maupassant** by *Guy de Maupassant*   ISBN: 1-59462-157-8   **$16.95**
"For days and days, nights and nights, I had dreamed of that first kiss which was to consecrate our engagement, and I knew not on what spot I should put my lips..."   Fiction/Classics Pages 240

☐ **The Art of Cross-Examination** by *Francis L. Wellman*   ISBN: 1-59462-309-0   **$26.95**
Written by a renowned trial lawyer, Wellman imparts his experience and uses case studies to explain how to use psychology to extract desired information through questioning.   How-to/Science/Reference Pages 408

☐ **Answered or Unanswered?** by *Louisa Vaughan*   ISBN: 1-59462-248-5   **$10.95**
Miracles of Faith in China   Religion Pages 112

☐ **The Edinburgh Lectures on Mental Science (1909)** by *Thomas*   ISBN: 1-59462-008-3   **$11.95**
This book contains the substance of a course of lectures recently given by the writer in the Queen Street Hall, Edinburgh. Its purpose is to indicate the Natural Principles governing the relation between Mental Action and Material Conditions...   New Age/Psychology Pages 148

☐ **Ayesha** by *H. Rider Haggard*   ISBN: 1-59462-301-5   **$24.95**
Verily and indeed it is the unexpected that happens! Probably if there was one person upon the earth from whom the Editor of this, and of a certain previous history, did not expect to hear again...   Classics Pages 380

☐ **Ayala's Angel** by *Anthony Trollope*   ISBN: 1-59462-352-X   **$29.95**
The two girls were both pretty, but Lucy who was twenty-one who supposed to be simple and comparatively unattractive, whereas Ayala was credited, as her Bombwhat romantic name might show, with poetic charm and a taste for romance. Ayala when her father died was nineteen...   Fiction Pages 484

☐ **The American Commonwealth** by *James Bryce*   ISBN: 1-59462-286-8   **$34.45**
An interpretation of American democratic political theory. It examines political mechanics and society from the perspective of Scotsman James Bryce   Politics Pages 572

☐ **Stories of the Pilgrims** by *Margaret P. Pumphrey*   ISBN: 1-59462-116-0   **$17.95**
This book explores pilgrims religious oppression in England as well as their escape to Holland and eventual crossing to America on the Mayflower, and their early days in New England...   History Pages 268

www.bookjungle.com email: sales@bookjungle.com fax: 630-214-0564 mail: Book Jungle PO Box 2226 Champaign, IL 61825

Title	ISBN	Price	QTY
The Fasting Cure by *Sinclair Upton* — In the Cosmopolitan Magazine for May, 1910, and in the Contemporary Review (London) for April, 1910, I published an article dealing with my experiences in fasting. I have written a great many magazine articles, but never one which attracted so much attention... *New Age/Self Help/Health Pages 164*	1-59462-222-1	$13.95	
Hebrew Astrology by *Sepharial* — In these days of advanced thinking it is a matter of common observation that we have left many of the old landmarks behind and that we are now pressing forward to greater heights and to a wider horizon than that which represented the mind-content of our progenitors... *Astrology Pages 144*	1-59462-308-2	$13.45	
Thought Vibration or The Law of Attraction in the Thought World by *William Walker Atkinson* — *Psychology/Religion Pages 144*	1-59462-127-6	$12.95	
Optimism by *Helen Keller* — Helen Keller was blind, deaf, and mute since 19 months old, yet famously learned how to overcome these handicaps, communicate with the world, and spread her lectures promoting optimism. An inspiring read for everyone... *Biographies/Inspirational Pages 84*	1-59462-108-X	$15.95	
Sara Crewe by *Frances Burnett* — In the first place, Miss Minchin lived in London. Her home was a large, dull, tall one, in a large, dull square, where all the houses were alike, and all the sparrows were alike, and where all the door-knockers made the same heavy sound... *Childrens/Classic Pages 88*	1-59462-360-0	$9.45	
The Autobiography of Benjamin Franklin by *Benjamin Franklin* — The Autobiography of Benjamin Franklin has probably been more extensively read than any other American historical work, and no other book of its kind has had such ups and downs of fortune. Franklin lived for many years in England, where he was agent... *Biographies/History Pages 332*	1-59462-135-7	$24.95	

Name	
Email	
Telephone	
Address	
City, State ZIP	

☐ Credit Card   ☐ Check / Money Order

Credit Card Number	
Expiration Date	
Signature	

Please Mail to: Book Jungle
PO Box 2226
Champaign, IL 61825
or Fax to: 630-214-0564

ORDERING INFORMATION

web: *www.bookjungle.com*
email: *sales@bookjungle.com*
fax: *630-214-0564*
mail: *Book Jungle PO Box 2226 Champaign, IL 61825*
or PayPal *to sales@bookjungle.com*

Please contact us for bulk discounts

DIRECT-ORDER TERMS

20% Discount if You Order Two or More Books
Free Domestic Shipping!
Accepted: Master Card, Visa, Discover, American Express

www.ingramcontent.com/pod-product-compliance
Lightning Source LLC
Chambersburg PA
CBHW081325040426
42453CB00013B/2308